Walk Around

A Farming Town

Peter and Connie Roop

Heinemann Library
Des Plaines, Illinois

Designed by Lindaanne Donohoe
Printed in Hong Kong

03 02 01 00 99
10 9 8 7 6 5 4 3 2

Library of Congress Cataloging-in-Publication Data

Roop, Peter.
    A farming town / Peter and Connie Roop.
        p.   cm. — (Walk around)
    Includes bibliographical references and index.
    Summary: Uses Wilton, North Dakota, as an example to introduce
farm towns through distinguishing characteristics such as their
homes, schools, stores, means of transportation, and place of
employment.
    ISBN 1-57572-127-9 (lib. bdg.)
    1. Cities and towns—United States—Juvenile literature. 2. North
Dakota—Rural conditions—Juvenile literature.   [1. Cities and
towns. 2. North Dakota.] I. Roop, Connie. II. Title.
III. Series: Roop, Peter. Walk around.
HT123.R6473   1998
307.72'0973—dc21   98-14917
                                                                            CIP
                                                                            AC

Acknowledgments
All photographs by Phil Martin except those listed below.

Cover photograph: Phil Martin

The author and publishers are grateful to the following for permission to reproduce
copyright photographs:

Michael Carpenter, p. 4 (Harvard); ©Tony Stone Images/Glen Allison, p. 5 (Strafford).

Special thanks to Bud Veis

Every effort has been made to contact copyright holders of any material reproduced
in this book. Any omissions will be rectified in subsequent printings if notice is given
to the publisher.

Some words are shown in bold, **like this.** You can find out what they mean by looking
in the glossary.

For Mother, who took her first steps in Wilton. Long may your journey continue.

Contents

What Is a Farming Town?

near Mead, Washington

Harvard, Illinois

A farming town is a town in the country that is the center of a farming **community**. Farming towns are different sizes and provide different services. Some farming communities have hundreds of people. Others have thousands of people.

Wilton, North Dakota

Strafford, Vermont

Mapping the Farming Town

A farming **community** is made up of a town and the farms that surround the town. Farming communities are spread out over great distances. Most **citizens** of a farming community know each other.

This map shows the farming community of Wilton, North Dakota, the area you will walk around in this book. A little more than a thousand people live in this community. The nearest city is Bismarck. It is about 30 miles (48 km) from Wilton. Around 50 thousand people live in Bismarck.

Wilton

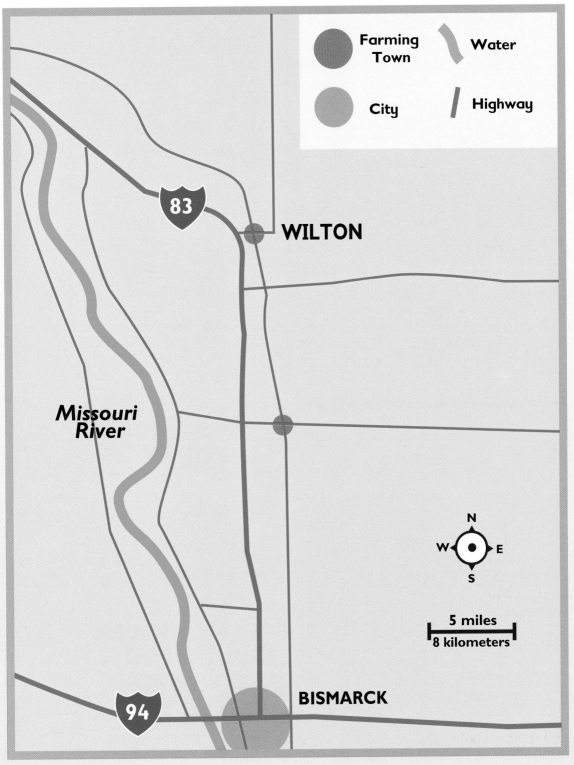

Legend:
- Farming Town
- City
- Water
- Highway

83

WILTON

Missouri River

N
W · E
S

5 miles
8 kilometers

94

BISMARCK

Homes

People in a farming **community** live in many kinds of homes. Some people live in apartments above a store in town. Some people who live outside of town live in **mobile homes.**

Many families live in houses in or near town. They have front and back yards and may have farmland all around. Outside of town, many families live on large farms.

Getting Around

Most people drive cars and trucks because places are often far away. For short trips in town, many people walk or ride bikes.

Most farm towns are near railroads.

Railroads move **crops** and other farming

products to and from markets. A tall **grain**

elevator is usually near the railroad.

Schools

In some farming **communities,** elementary, middle school or junior high, and high school are in the same building. Most farming communities do not have many students. It is easier to have all the students in one building.

Some children live far from school. Many kids go to school in a neighboring town because nearby towns often share schools. These students ride buses to get to school.

The Police

In a farming **community,** there is only one police station. There are only a few police officers. Police stations in many towns are in a city hall or government building.

Police in neighboring farming communities help each other. **County** police forces also help the small farming communities when needed.

Working

Most **citizens** in a farming **community** work in **agriculture.** Many people are farmers. Others sell farm machines or help farmers sell **grain** or farm animals.

Some people work in stores in town or help
run the town. A few people **commute**
to work in bigger towns or cities.

Shopping

Many stores in a farming town are on a **main street.** These stores sell some of the everyday things people need, such as food and gas for cars and farm machines.

Other stores are on a highway or busy road that goes out of town. Sometimes people have to go to a bigger town to buy everything they need. Many people grow some of their own food in their gardens at home.

The Library

A farming town may not have its own library. Some towns share a library with other small towns nearby. Some farm **communities** may have a **bookmobile.**

Charles B. Ph...
LIBRA[R...
Hours: MON—FRI 3:30–5...
Sign in Memory o...
OTTO & PEARL AND[E...

Bookmobiles and town libraries may not
have everything people want. Librarians
can ask other libraries to send the things
people need. People can also use computers
to get information from all over the world.

Banks and Money

There may be only one bank in a farming **community.** This bank has a drive-up window where people do their banking while waiting in their cars. Some people go inside or use a cash machine to get money.

Bankers help the community by **lending** money. They lend money to farmers so they can buy new machines. Stores borrow money from banks to buy more products to sell.

The Post Office

There is one post office in a farming **community.** It is usually a small building. People go to the post office to mail special packages or pick up their mail.

Letter carriers must deliver mail to farms and homes outside of town. They drive specially-built cars to make their job easier.

Playing

People spend much of their time with family and friends. Some meet each day to talk. Others go fishing together. There are many outdoor activities to do in and around a farming **community**—alone or with others.

Some farming communities have fairs each year. Others may have a **rodeo.** Many farming towns are very proud of their school sports teams. **Citizens** enjoy watching the games and cheering for their teams.

Helping Out

Most people in a farming **community** live far apart. Many communities are small and don't have many services. People **rely** on each other for help and friendship.

Some children visit **senior citizens.** The children bring their favorite books to share. Senior citizens share stories and teach the children about their community. Spending time together helps build a more caring community.

Glossary

agriculture farming or raising farm animals

bookmobile bus that carries library books around town

citizens people who live in a town or community

community area where people live, work, and shop

commute to travel from home to work and back

county areas that states are divided into

crops foods grown on farms

grain seeds from cereal plants such as corn

grain elevator building for keeping grain

lending letting someone use something that will be returned later

main street most important street in town

mobile homes homes that can be moved

rely to get help from someone

rodeo contest in which people test their skills at riding horses and roping cattle

senior citizens elderly people

More Books to Read

Florian, Douglas. *A Year in the Country.*
New York: Greenwillow, 1989.

Kallen, Stuart. *The Farm.* Minneapolis, Minn:
Abdo & Daughters, 1997.

Provensen, Alice and Martin. *Town and
Country.* Orlando, Fla: Browndeer Press
(Harcourt Brace), 1994.

Whelan, Gloria. *Bringing the Farmhouse
Home.* New York: Simon & Schuster
Children's, 1992.

Index